Kafka's Soup

A complete history of world literature
in 14 recipes

Kafka's Soup

A complete history of world literature
in 14 recipes

Written and illustrated by
Mark Crick

**Wakefield
Press**

Wakefield Press
1 The Parade West
Kent Town
South Australia 5067
www.wakefieldpress.com.au

Published by arrangement with Libri Publications Ltd, London

First published in Australia and New Zealand 2006
Text and illustrations copyright © Mark Crick, 2006

Typeset by Clinton Ellicott, Wakefield Press
Printed in China at Everbest Printing Co. Ltd

ISBN 1 86254 710 6

Government of South Australia
Arts SA

fox creek

Contents

Lamb with Dill Sauce

à la Raymond Chandler

1 kg lean leg of lamb, cut into large chunks
1 onion, sliced
1 carrot, cut into sticks
1 tablespoon crushed dill seeds, or 3–4 sprigs fresh dill
1 bay leaf
12 peppercorns
1/2 teaspoon salt
850 ml chicken stock
50 g butter
1 tablespoon plain flour
1 egg yolk
3 tablespoons cream
2 teaspoons lemon juice

I sipped on my whisky sour, ground out my cigarette on the
chopping board and watched a bug trying to crawl out of the
basin. I needed a table at Maxim's, a hundred bucks and a
gorgeous blonde; what I had was a leg of lamb and no clues.
I took hold of the joint. It felt cold and damp, like a coroner's
handshake. I took out a knife and cut the lamb into pieces.
Feeling the blade in my hand I sliced an onion, and before
I knew what I was doing a carrot lay in pieces on the slab.
None of them moved. I threw the lot into a pan with a bunch
of dill stalks, a bay leaf, a handful of peppercorns and a pinch

Lamb with Dill Sauce

of salt. They had it coming to them, so I covered them with chicken stock and turned up the heat. I wanted them to boil slowly, just about as slowly as anything can boil. An hour and a half and a half-pint of bourbon later they weren't so tough and neither was I. I separated the meat from the vegetables and covered it to keep it moist. The knife was still in my hand but I couldn't hear any sirens.

In this town the grease always rises to the top, so I strained the juice and skimmed off the fat. I added more water and put it back on the heat. It was time to deal with the butter and flour, so I mixed them together into a paste and added it to the stock. There wasn't a whisk, so using my blackjack I beat out any lumps until the paste was smooth.

It started to boil, so I let it simmer for two minutes.

I roughed up the egg yolk and cream and mixed in some of the hot sauce before putting the lot back into the pan. I put the squeeze on a lemon and it soon juiced. It was easy. It was much too easy, but I knew if I let the sauce boil the yolk was gonna scramble.

By now I was ready to pour the sauce over the meat and serve, but I wasn't hungry. The blonde hadn't showed. She was smarter than I thought. I went outside to poison myself, with cigarettes and whisky.

Tarragon Eggs
à la Jane Austen

4 eggs
2 teaspoons tarragon (fresh or dried)
40 g butter
pinch of salt
ground pepper

It is a truth universally acknowledged that eggs, kept for too long, go off. The eggs of Oakley Farm had only recently been settled in the kitchen at Somercote, but already Mrs B—— was planning a meal that would introduce them to the neighbourhood with what she hoped would be universal acceptance. Her eggs had been strongly endowed by nature with a turn for being uniformly agreeable and she hoped to see at least a half dozen of them make fine matches in the coming week. The arrival of a newcomer in the parish presented the perfect opportunity and Mrs B—— wasted no time in sending out invitations to a luncheon.

Many hours had been spent discussing the merits of one dish over another with her neighbour, Lady Cumberland. The two ladies took prodigious care when considering the advantages of tea over coffee and whether the toast should be white or brown, subjects on which Lady Cumberland delivered her opinions in so decisive a manner that Mrs B—— dared not disagree. Lady Cumberland was no

The Perfect Union of Miss Egg and Monsieur Astragon

After Rowlandson

Tarragon Eggs

supporter of the new cooking, which she blamed, first, for bringing ingredients of obscure origin into undue distinction, and secondly, for raising cooks to honours of which their fathers and grandfathers had never dreamt. As a sacrifice to propriety, Mrs B—— agreed that the dish would be a traditional one.

With the day of the luncheon drawing near, Mrs B—— was suffering terribly with her nerves. The event that she had announced with such anticipation had ceased to be a source of pleasure. On the contrary, it was unfair of the local ladies to allow the burden of organising such gatherings to fall so often to her; and was it not strange that Mrs Eliot had not returned the courtesy of the dinner that she had given a fortnight past? Such were the mutterings of Mrs B—— as she paced the garden seeking inspiration, when the sound of a carriage crossing the lawn announced the arrival of Lady Cumberland, who suggested a small rehearsal. So it was that the two neighbours found themselves in the kitchen at Somercote, still busily searching for a proper suitor for the eggs. While Lady Cumberland sat drinking tea, Mrs B—— chose for her employment to search the pantry, stalking the absent suitor.

"Parsley might do," said she. The herb was a regular at the house and the chance that it might combine well with her eggs meant that Mrs B—— could only think well of it:

"Good-looking, with an easy and unaffected manner."
Lady Cumberland's reaction was unequivocal: "Too much
curl to its leaf, and too often seen in great bunches at
fishmongers. It would be a most unhappy connection."

Mrs B—— was not used to disagreeing with the better
informed mind of Lady Cumberland, and now, her every
cherished opinion of parsley's worth overthrown, she turned
her eye to rarer visitors, including the tarragon. She had
always thought tarragon a difficult herb and hard to please.
"It refuses to grow here, it refuses to grow there, but fancies
itself so very great, disappearing every winter I know not
where. I quite detest the plant."

"French tarragon is an aristocrat among herbs, and
although I think it too good for your eggs, I cannot deny that
it would be a fine match for them," said Lady Cumberland.
Mrs B—— received the remark with all the forbearance of
civility and the slight on her eggs went unremarked. But a
recommendation from so high a source as Lady Cumberland
could not be ignored, and Mrs B——'s contempt for the
noble tarragon was soon forgotten. The possibility that her
eggs might find themselves cooked with the aristocratic
herb sent Mrs B—— into such a state of excitement that
Lady Cumberland would have risen to leave were it not for
the promise of luncheon. Instead she instructed her host to
produce the dish without delay: "I suggest you begin."

Tarragon Eggs

Mrs B—— obliged by beating the eggs slightly to break up yolks and whites. On Lady Cumberland's instruction she then passed the eggs through a sieve to remove the thread and further mix the white and yolk without creating the froth that can be "so unsightly". No sooner had such an end been reached than she added the tarragon, which was by now high in her good graces. She could barely hold back her raptures at how good the tarragon and eggs looked together and anticipated the happy moment when she would see them united, on toast.

Taking half the butter, Mrs B—— spread it around the pan, and pronounced it to be the most tractable of ingredients. The remaining butter she added in small lumps to the mixture, together with salt and pepper, before cooking the whole over a gentle heat, stirring constantly and scraping the bottom of the pan as she did so. As soon as the attachment seemed to strengthen she removed the dish from the heat and kept stirring; the warmth of the pan was sufficient to complete the cooking before the eggs became too dry.

This delightful union Mrs B—— then served with toasted bread, and with so much good taste and true merit that, when Lady Cumberland was obliged to declare the dish acceptable, the happiness of her guests was assured. And so it proved to be the case, with the possible exception of Mrs Eliot, who, when she detailed the particulars to her husband, remarked on the lack of finery or parade in the table setting and on the inferiority of the dish next to her own eggs benedict. But, in spite of all these deficiencies, the hopes, the sensitivities and the appetites of the small band of true friends who gathered for luncheon were fully answered in the perfect success of the union.

Quick Miso Soup
à la Franz Kafka

4–5 small mushrooms
3 dessertspoons fermented miso
150 g silken tofu
a few leaves of dried wakame
soy sauce

K. recognised that if a man is not always on his guard this
kind of thing can happen. He was looking into the refrigerator
and found it to be almost completely bare, apart from some
mushrooms, which he began to slice. His guests sat waiting
at the table and yet he appeared to have little to offer them.
Whether he had invited them or whether they had arrived
uninvited was not clear. If it were the first case he was angry
with himself for failing to engage a cook for the evening so
that he might command some authority at the table; for now
his visitors were looking towards him as though he were a
subordinate whose inefficiency was delaying their dinner. But
in the second case they could hardly expect to be fed, arriving
unexpectedly at such a time. The sound of a kettle boiling
brought his attention back to the food and at the same time
he noticed a jar of fermented miso and a block of silken tofu,
perhaps left by his landlady. He placed three spoonfuls of the
miso into a saucepan and poured on two pints of hot water,
shielding the process from the panel as he did so. He became

Soup

Quick Miso Soup

angry with himself for thinking of the new arrivals as a panel; they had not announced their purpose in calling on him and as yet he did not know what position each of them held. Their manner suggested, perhaps, that they were higher officials but it was also quite possible that he was their superior and they were calling on him merely to create a good impression.

With shame K. realised that he had not offered his guests anything to drink, but when he looked up he saw that a bottle was open on the table and the judges were already enjoying his wine. He found it abominable that they had served themselves without permission, but he knew their impertinence was not without significance. K. decided to shame them for their rudeness. "How is the wine?", he called. But the ruse backfired. "It would be better with some food," they chorused. "But since you have not even granted us the courtesy of dressing for dinner we do not have high hopes." K. could scarcely believe it as he noticed with discomfort that he was, indeed, in shirt and drawers.

When the soup was simmering, K. cut the tofu into one-centimetre cubes and dropped it into the steaming pan with the mushrooms and wakame. Looking out of the window into the darkness he noticed that a girl was watching from the neighbouring house. The girl's severe expression was not unattractive to K., but the thought that she was deriving some pleasure from his situation sent him into a fury and he struck the worktop with his fist. It occurred to him that she might in some way be attached to the interrogation commission or could influence his case, and he looked beseechingly towards her, but she had backed away now and he might already have thrown away any advantages that his situation bestowed upon him. In two minutes the soup was ready. K. poured it into bowls and served his visitors. One of the four chairs around the table had been removed and, not without discomfort, K. saw that the panel was making no effort to make room for him. He added a splash of soy sauce to each of the bowls while the elder of the three judges addressed the others as if K. were invisible. "He needs to rid himself of a great many illusions; it's possible he imagines that we are subordinates calling on him to win his approval."

K.'s feeling that he was an outsider at his own dinner party was not unfamiliar. He was sorry that he was not dressed in his grey suit: its elegant cut had caused a sensation among his friends, and it was of the utmost importance to create a good impression in these situations.

It was essential for a man in his position not to appear surprised by events and, as the interrogation commission divided the contents of K's bowl between them, K. stood still and tried to collect himself, for he knew that great demands would be made upon him and the soup might yet influence the outcome of his case.

Rich Chocolate Cake

à la Irvine Welsh

250 g butter
500 g sugar
40 g cocoa
150 g milk chocolate
250 ml coffee
2 eggs
275 g self-raising flour
375 ml port

For the icing:
200 g dark chocolate
100 g caster sugar
100 ml double cream
100 ml kahlua (optional)

Ah make ma way back to the shithole that ah call home,
wi aw the gear ah need, but ah kin barely move. Ma heid is
throbbing like it's aboot tae burst, showering passers-by wi
brain and bone, and ah'm so fuckin frail ma legs could snap
as ah climb the stairs. Ah hope nae fucker's seen me coming
back. Ah dinnae want to share any of this shite wi ma so-called
friends.

Ah drop a packet of butter intae the pan and light the
flame beneath it. As it melts, ah pour on the sugar, watching

Plate 6.

After Hogarth

A Quality Fuckin' Cook Up

Rich Chocolate Cake

the white grains dissolve intae the golden brown liquid. They're dissolving cleanly; it's good fuckin shite. Ma hands are shaking as ah sprinkle the brown powder of the cocoa intae the pan and when ah drop in the bar of chocolate ah have the satisfaction of watching it melt straight away. This is a quality fuckin cook-up.

As the mixture begins to bubble and spit ah find ah'm oot of coffee, but a quick scramble under the settee produces a mug of the stuff and ah'm no fuckin goin back doon those stairs. Intae the brew it goes. The pain in ma heid is beginning to subside and, what wi the smell of the gear cookin and the calming site of the gas flame, ah'm feeling better already.

Ah take the pan off the heat while ah crack two eggs into a jug. Ma eyes focus long enough oan the shells tae read the crack by date: the bastards want me tae throw them oot and buy more. Mebbe the hen that laid them is sitting in the freezer doon at Scotmid, but ah know they keep for months. There's nae need tae beat the eggs: the 14.22 from Kings Cross goes by the windae and stirs every fuckin thing, including me. Ah measure oot the flour and at the sight of such a mountain of white powder ah'm tempted tae stick ma nose in. Ah add the eggs and flour to the mixture and pour oan a drop of port. Ah hae a drop masel; it's no bad, so ah put some more intae the pan. The bottle's soon finished.

Ah've drunk half and the other half's goan intae the mixture – greedy fuckin cake.

There's a knock at the door. Fuck. Ah ignore it. Ma heid is beginning tae throb again and ah decide it's time tae hit the bevvies. Ah've enough cans of special tae see me through till the cookin's over, if nae fucker comes in. The knocking starts again, only this time it's louder.

– Stevie, ah know yer in there, open the fucking door.

It's Spanner, ma so-called best mate. No way am ah sharing any of this gear wi him, but he's gaunnae take the door off the hinges. Ah open up.

– Moan in Span, it's guid tae see yer. Can you spot me a twenty til ma giro arrives in the mornin.

It nearly fucking works. He's aboot tae turn round, but his nose must still contain some traces of functionality, because he starts sniffin the air like a dug.

– Yer cookin up, Stevie. Ah kin tell.

He goes straight in tae the kitchen and by the time ah've closed the door he's opened one of ma cans and is holding his heid over the pan, breathing deeply. What kin ye do?

There's a mountain of the brown stuff in the pan, so ah grease two cake tins and pour the mixture in. Ah can hardly wait. Ah'm tempted to eat it as it is, but the last thing ah need is a fuckin bad chocolate trip. The tins go intae the oven at 200 degrees. Ah cook everything at the same temperature;

Rich Chocolate Cake

ah fuckin hate those yuppie bastards with their fan assisted bollocks and temperatures. When you're cookin, you're cookin, end ay fuckin story.

– How long Stevie?

Spanner's as desperate as ah am.

– Aboot an hour.

– Kin it be quicker?

– Ah'm cookin as fast as ah can and yer nae fuckin help.

Spanner's aboot as much use in the kitchen as an amputated prick at a hoor's convention, an ah can tell he's been oan the bevvies. While he's away for a pish, ah put the dark chocolate in a pan and measure oot the caster sugar.

Ah add the cream and kahlua tae the pan. Kahlua's a fuckin lassie's drink, ah know, but it's no bad in a cake. When ah go tae the scales for the sugar Spanner's already there, aboot tae start shovelling the white powder up his hooter. I dinnae shout stop, but the penny soon drops. He's greetin like hell as he sticks his nose under the tap, while ah'm stirring the sugar into the pan.

Ah kin hear someone calling ma name. For a moment ah think it's a voice in ma heid, calling me back to planet earth, but ah soon catch on. It's another fucking unwelcome visitor. They'll go soon enough; but Spanner, ever useless, opens the windae and shouts down. Hiddy and Gav are standing in the street, suited and booted. They both work for Grenson's the undertakers, and the two cunts have come around in the company car. Ah owe Gav a fifty and he's no one tae forget. What does he expect? Gav and Hiddy are the only poor fuckers tae get a job, since the social caught em signing on fer five different addresses. They'll no be riding the giro d'ecosse for a while.

– Stevie's cooking up.

Ah'm tempted tae lift Span's feet and tip him oot the windae, the big mouthed cunt, but ah dinnae have the strength. Gav and Hiddy are soon at the door with what sounds like a battering ram. Spanner lets them in, while ah grab another can of heavy before those greedy bastards drink the lot. Gav staggers in looking the man, in a black suit and tie.

– How long Stevie? We've got tae nash.

Hiddy is behind him and between them they're carrying a fuckin coffin.

– Sorry Stevie, the last time we left the car it wis stolen. We got the car back but the body wis missing. It's the sack if we lose another.

Hiddy kin barely breathe. The effort of climbing the stairs has nearly finished him off. They dump the box on the floor and Hiddy collapses into a chair, the skin on his face stretched like cling film over his skull. He could swap places with the man in the box and you'd no notice the difference.

Rich Chocolate Cake

Ah go to close the door and see a wee lassie standing in the hall. She's wearing a black coat five sizes too big and her face is as white as a sheet. Ah look at Gav.

– Aw Stevie, this is Debbie. That's her boyfriend in the box. We'll no be long, Debbie, moan in.

She has the look of one of those lassies whae'll do anything tae please. She isn't makin any fuss aboot her boyfriend's little detour on his way to his last resting place, that's fer sure. She sits oan the settee hugging hersel. She's nae bad, she won't be oan her puff for long. Ah'll fuckin move in there, pretty sharpish an aw. Then ah notice she's nae hugging hersel; she's holding a bairn under that big coat. It starts greetin and she gets oot one of her tits tae feed it. The cheeky slut's only breast-feeding, in ma hoose. Ah what the fuck, ah've got tae finish the icing. Gav and Hiddy hae forgotten their hurry and are hittin the bevvies, their feet up on Debbie's boyfriend's wooden overcoat. If it fits him like Debbie's coat fits her, the poor bastard must've been a midget.

The hour is nearly up. Ah warm through the icing and remove the cake tins from the cooker. Ah find a syringe and needle, ideal for checking the middle of the cake is cooked. Nae problem, the needle is clean. Oan the outside the cake is burnt, so ah cut off the burnt bits and slap on the icing while it's still hot. The two slabs sit there glistening, like bars of brown bullion. Spanner has by now drunk the rest of the kahlua, and is oot of his box, jumping around desperate for a piece of the brown stuff. He can fuckin wait. Ah'm feeling sorry for the wee lassie so she'll come first – after me, of course. The crowd are all smiles as ah come into the room wi a big plate of chocolate salvation, and Debbie's boyfriend makes a nice wee coffee table.

We're all soon stuffing our faces, though ah would'nae recommend the heavy as the ideal accompaniment. Wee Debbie is getting in the swing. She's put the bairn oan the floor wi a piece of cake to stop his greeting and she's cramming a piece of the dark slice intae her gob, her eyes rolling back in her head, like if she eats enough chocolate it'll stop all the pain. Spanner, as usual, has overdone it. The kahlua does nae mix well with the heavy, the cake and whativir he had before he arrived. He's back at the windae; who the fuck is arriving now? But he's no talking; he's spewing intae the street, lazy fuck. Spanner is the original come-back kid, and two minutes later he picks up the last piece of cake.

– It's no bad – he says – But it's no the same as skag.

No bad? The fucker's eaten huf of it.

Gav and Hiddy are back on their feet, struggling tae pick up their quiet friend.

– Thanks Stevie, we've got tae nash, says Gav – Don't forget that fifty you owe us.

Rich Chocolate Cake

Ah'm just in time to remove a plate from the coffee table before it's repossessed, and they're away. But ah've goat Debbie's address. Ah look oot the windae: down below they make a pretty wee procession, all in black, weaving from side to side, like Archie Gemmill in slow motion. But the car's no looking too good. Spanner's scored a direct hit. It looks like some fucker's tried tae give the car a chocolate icing, but Gav and Hiddy dinnae notice and they're soon loaded up and off. What kin ye do? He's no the first person tae be carried in and oot of ma place. Nor is he the first to drive off covered with vomit. But credit tae him, he's brought something new tae the game, the poor bastard. Don't get me wrong, ah dinnae feel sorry for him, ah'll be following in his footsteps soon enough. Ah'm the one ah feel sorry fer. What am ah doing that's so fuckin new? We think we're the centre of the universe, but we're not. What's the universe anyway? It's just a great big fuckin roundaboot that we're all going round endlessly and there's nothing we kin do aboot it. We live we die. End of fuckin story.

Tiramisu

à la Marcel Proust

2 cups cold coffee
Amaretto di Saronno
12–15 savoiardi sponge fingers
4 eggs
100 g caster sugar
500 g mascarpone
cocoa powder

Although the fashionableness of any café and its degree
of comfort usually stand in inverse relation to each other,
on a cold day in March I found myself on the Boulevard
Beaumarchais, in a café, whose owners, from their
headquarters no doubt far from the district in which I now
sat, had succeeded in finding the precise median such that
the establishment offered neither style nor comfort; its
combination of brown sofas, blonde wood and red walls
looked like it had been delivered in a single packing case,
from a world which knew nothing of the one to which it was
expediting its wares, the result being a mediocrity so well
researched that it shouted its presence. Looking now at the
cappuccino served to me in the crude white mug, the surface
of which had been whipped into a frenzy of froth and too
liberally sprinkled with chocolate, I lamented the fact that
my age now required me to stop and rest when my body

Tiramisu

demanded it and not when my eyes were attracted by something or someone too tempting to resist. Yet when I sipped at the beverage, suddenly the memory appeared; the chocolate powder sprinkled on my cappuccino became the cocoa on the surface of the tiramisu that I had first tasted one evening in the garden at Combray, where my father was holding a small party to welcome the former ambassador to Rome, who had recently returned to the neighbourhood with his daughter.

From this ancient past – its great houses gone and its inhabitants dwindling, like the last creatures of a mythical forest – came something infinitely more frail and yet more alive, insubstantial yet persistent; the memories of smell and taste, so faithful, resisted the destruction and rebuilt for a moment the palace wherein dwelt the remembrance of that evening and of that tiramisu.

The combination of cream and coffee seemed to offer access to a world more real than that in which I sat, this pretender that announced itself the 'home of coffee', whose distinct signage of 'Simply Delicious', 'Come in for Lunch', 'Hot Panini' called to a generation to whom I was lost. Did any of its clientele know of the beauty of the Café Florian on St Mark's Square where my ancestors had once taken coffee with Byron? The memory gone, I sipped again at the hot beverage; once more the recollection came of that first

Tiramisu

experience, the evening at Combray when I was introduced to Ursula Patrignani, her body flexing like a prima ballerina, bowing in a show of mock courtesy as she handed me a small bowl of tiramisu, and of the slight dizziness I felt in her presence as I looked at the movement of her exquisite Botticelli mouth, too dazed to hear her words. The very unsteadiness of my legs became the rocking of a gondola, as we docked at a Venetian palazzo and walked arm in arm through the mist into a room graced by Bellini's 'Feast of the Gods'. Again the memory faded, and the decaying eau-de-nil walls of the palazzo and the works of the Venetian masters were replaced by red and brown panels and over-enlarged photographs depicting young people in casual dress drinking coffee. I feared that the recipe was lost to me forever.

The creamy draught had cooled; its flavour seemed to be dying already and with it remembrance of that evening. Sensing that the memories had not departed forever and were lingering like souls after death, I ordered a second cup of the milky drink which might in other circumstances have disgusted me; now I craved it as if it were the elixir of youth and capable of curing my old age. "The same, Monsieur?" asked the young waitress. "I am sorry but before I gave you one flavoured with almond syrup by mistake." The poor girl looked anxious, but I nearly kissed those delicate white hands of hers from gratitude; it was the sweet almond taste that had awoken that beauty from its sleep in the dark forest of past memory, recalling the Amaretto di Saronno that I had tasted for the first time that night with Ursula Patrignani in the gaslight among the chrysanthemums. The waitress smiled as she served what was for her just another drink, but for me the liquid was a hallucinatory potion that could open the doors of my perception; her consciousness had barely registered my presence because I was only partly in her world, choosing to probe this portal to truths which dwelt in a realm more real than hers.

This time I closed my eyes and sipped deeply of the draught, realising that what I sought dwelt not in the cappuccino but within myself. This white-hooded potion was my guide down to the underworld, and would assist in shaking free the anchor that kept these elusive memories so firmly held in the depths of my consciousness.

Separate from the others we now talked; hidden by the chrysanthemums, and knowing that no one could see how foolish I must look, I gathered my courage, resolving to ask her to marry me there and then, but as I opened my mouth to speak she gently fed to me a teaspoonful of the delightful mixture, and I was silenced. Never before had I accepted to take food in such a way except from my mother as she gave me my medicine before kissing me goodnight. As I swallowed the heavenly concoction I found myself imbued with an unknown

Tiramisu

courage; I had to make her understand what I was feeling. "I am experiencing something that I have never felt before," I told her, but before I could continue, she spoke. "I know, it happens to everyone the first time. Chef's tiramisu is simply sublime; Father says that it has saved us from a thousand international incidents and that without it he could never have maintained a peaceful Europe. Madame Verdurin has tried everything to get the recipe, but Father wouldn't give it even to the Duke of Milan." My feelings for her were so intense that I grew light-headed, confused my thoughts with my speech and became unsure of what I had said out loud or thought to myself. Did she feel anything for me? Could she find it in her heart to reciprocate the profound feelings that I had for her? Involuntarily I cried out, "I must know." Whether she really misunderstood me or coquettishly chose to interpret my question in such a way as to keep alive the tantalising doubt that made my mind so feverish, she continued, "You shall know. Chef begins always with the coffee, fresh and strong, but chilled in ice, so that it doesn't dissolve the savoiardi, the little sponge fingers that are sent regularly from Italy. These he dips into the coffee, turning them, before laying them in the bowl to form the foundation for his creation. The secret is that he always laces the coffee with the amaretto, which he keeps at hand throughout the process." I could barely remain on my feet. "He then takes the eggs and separates out the yolks, which he mixes with sugar to form a soft cream. The whites he whisks into a snowy peak." To throw myself from that snow-swept mountain. "He then reunites the two mixtures," oh blessed union, "before adding the mascarpone a little at a time and a final splash of the amaretto. He then spreads the creamy concoction on top of the sponge fingers and continues with alternating layers until the last layer of cream, which he covers with cocoa powder shaken from the sieve, taking care not to miss an inch." At this I staggered backwards and fainted.

When I recovered consciousness I was in my bed at Combray, my mother touching my shoulder to wake me. At the touch of her hand I looked up. "I'm sorry, monsieur, but would you mind moving to a smaller table?" A group of young mothers with perambulators waited in the doorway, looking towards me. My cup sat empty on the table and I walked out onto the busy Parisian boulevard.

Coq au Vin

à la Gabriel Garcia Marquez

1 whole chicken, c. 3 1/2 kg
ingredients for marinade – see page 39
olive oil
800 g baby onions
200 g smoked pork
2 carrots
5 cloves of garlic
3 sticks of celery
3 leeks
a few leaves of sage

Father Antonio del Sacrament del Altar Castaneda sat in the garden and watched the afternoon die. The darkness had begun to grow as heavy as the heat, and he held off going into the inferno of the house as long as he could. But he had smoked his last cigar and was now unarmed as the mosquitoes enveloped him, and he was forced to retreat into the gaslit interior.

The light of the kitchen dazzled him as he closed the door on the swarm. He slapped his neck, killing a winged intruder before it could feast, and reflected on the last rites. Earlier that day he had visited the murderer Fidel Agosto Santiago to hear his confession, but the prisoner had declared himself unready. Santiago would eat his last supper the following night, and since the condemned man refused to accept food from his

wife, the priest had taken on the responsibility. He sprayed the room with insecticide and began to cough.

Guiltily he looked across at Tobaga, the haughty mulatta who had prepared his evening meal every night for the last fifteen years. Watching her in the kitchen was a pleasure he had denied himself in his more venereal years, but that appetite was now a faint glow whose embers' warmth would only be extinguished by any attempt to refuel them. As she washed her hands he felt the need to urinate and left the room. His once powerful flow, which had reverberated in the night bucket with the sound of a stallion galloping, was reduced to a trickle, the intense ammonia smell of which rivalled the fumes that drifted in at dusk from the swamp and filled him with the sadness of decay.

When he returned to the kitchen Tobaga was preparing the marinade that would bathe the cockerel, that toughest of birds, for two days. "It is for Fidel. The Syrian's servant came today with the cockerel." The priest sat down and thought of the task that awaited him at the prison, but was startled from his thoughts by the sound of Tobaga chopping the bird into pieces. Each time she brought the cleaver down her dress swayed and the contours of her body made themselves more visible. She dropped the head into a bucket and Father Antonio felt a sharp prick on his neck, before bringing his hand down and killing the last survivor of the earlier siege.

à la Gabriel Garcia Marquez

Tobaga sliced two onions and added them to the cockerel in the pot. She covered the pieces with wine and, as they bathed in the blood-red liquid, she added juniper berries, coriander, mustard and pepper seeds, cloves and, finally, the rosemary and thyme. She then left the pot to marinate in the marble-lined pantry, the only cool place in the house, and one to which Father Antonio would retreat on afternoons of calamitous heat.

"When will the food be ready?" he asked.

"The marinade must be allowed to work for forty-eight hours," answered Tobaga.

"Can it be shorter?"

She looked at him, her eyes like golden almonds. "For a bird such as this?" And he knew it could not. The cockerel was a gift from the Syrian. Known as El Jaguarcito, The Little Jaguar, it had been the most successful of all his fighting birds. It had earned the Syrian a small fortune and its sacrifice was a mark of the debt he felt towards the condemned man. The priest turned a blind eye to the gambling and bloodshed of the cockfights but knew enough of El Jaguarcito's reputation to understand. "I will speak to the mayor in the morning."

Father Antonio rose, as he always did, at five, and dressed in darkness. Outside dawn struggled to rouse itself as he walked the short distance to the church. The carnivorous cloud

Coq au Vin

had descended once again and he raised the hood of his cassock until he was safely within the nave. As the worshippers arrived, each brought with them their own grief, an emptiness that dwarfed the nave. The insomniac was already there; it was rumoured that he had not slept for 75 years, except during Mass. The second to arrive was a woman who had recently lost her second son; like the first, he had been bitten by a rabid dog, but before the disease had been able to reach its violent zenith she had poisoned him. The last to arrive was the wife of the condemned man. The priest spoke without conviction and the Mass was brief. When the chance to leave came, pausing to remove a cockroach from the font, he headed in the direction of the mayor's house.

Like a marionette, whose strings might break at any moment, the town was stirring. A pair of black macaws flew overhead and the priest quickened his pace. A boy emerged from a temporary shelter at the side of the river and howled at the moon; he laughed at his joke and the priest shivered. Further on he overtook a family that appeared to be pushing all its belongings in a cart. A little girl led the way marching solemnly as she carried a vase of black peonies, and a boy at the rear of the family group held a cage which contained a white dove.

The mayor was half-dressed and sat with his braces over his bare shoulders. His wife did not greet the priest but silently poured coffee for the two men, looking on with her black-ringed eyes. "Thank God," said the mayor. "Another two hours before we start sweating again."

"I need a stay of execution." The priest said, without looking up from his coffee.

"Impossible. The soldiers are already on their way. They will arrive tomorrow."

"He has requested coq au vin and it will take two days to prepare."

"So it's true that the Syrian slaughtered El Jaguarcito?"

"El Jaguarcito is sitting in a pot in my kitchen."

The mayor crossed himself. "Can it not be cooked today?"

"Tobaga says it will be a crime before heaven. We cannot give Fidel Agosto Santiago a half-cooked last supper."

The mayor had no wish to disappoint Father Antonio or the condemned man, who had at one time been the greatest chef in the area. He sipped at his coffee and walked out onto the balcony. "If I agree, it will be to honour the Little Jaguar, not from sympathy for Fidel Santiago." Father Antonio knew that he had succeeded.

"Will you be at Mass on Sunday?" the priest asked as he was leaving.

"Say a prayer for me Father."

A troupial was singing as the priest headed for the prison. Fidel Santiago sat gambling with his guards. One of the

Coq au Vin

soldiers had lost his horse to the prisoner. The prison house was full of tobacco smoke and the priest coughed. When Father Antonio gave Fidel the news, the condemned man let out a deep sigh. "Tell her not to forget the sage, Father, just a few leaves."

The men returned to their gambling and the priest went out into the growing heat.

On the eve of the execution Father Antonio took up his position at the kitchen table and laid out the church accounts. Tobaga crossed herself, took the pieces of the Little Jaguar from the marinade and allowed them to drain. In a pan she heated the olive oil and added the small onions, whole. She chopped the smoked pork into small pieces and put that, too, into the pan. Into this last arena, slowly and with great circumspection, she now laid the pieces of the Little Jaguar. The body parts spat furiously as they touched the burning oil. When the flesh had turned golden Tobaga covered the carnage with the blood-red marinade and El Jaguarcito was silenced forever. She cut the carrots finely, her breasts making a little jump each time the blade struck the chopping board. The garlic cloves she left en chemise, their paper-dry covers like the sleeping pupae of butterflies that will never emerge. These she threw into the mixture, before adding the celery, leeks and seasoning. She covered the pan; the flames probed inquisitively at its base as she left it on a medium heat for an hour or so. His accounts untouched, Father Antonio closed his eyes and slipped into a siesta while Tobaga kept the vigil, never allowing the pan to run dry, constantly adding liquid from the marinade.

When the time came, Tobaga lifted the pieces of El Jaguarcito from the sauce. As she did so Father Antonio woke with a start. "Sleep on. I will wake you when it's ready," said Tobaga.

"I was dreaming that the food was poisoned and that the firing squad, refusing to be cheated, took me in his place."

"They may yet come for you."

Tobaga passed the sauce through a sieve, then, after touching the liquid and sucking on her finger, added more salt and continued to heat it. When she found the consistency she was seeking she returned the pieces of the cockerel to the liquid and added the sage leaves. A quarter of an hour later she woke the priest with a look. "The cockerel is ready," she said, and she saw the fear in his movements as he rose. "I can take the food to him, if you wish," she added.

"You can go later, but I will hear his confession first. He will not eat until his conscience is clear." And Father Antonio took up the dish and went out into the heat of the evening. As Tobaga watched him go she saw the carnivorous cloud descend to accompany him; the mosquitoes would feed as far as the prison.

Mushroom Risotto

à la John Steinbeck

25 g porcini mushrooms
extra virgin olive oil
3 field mushrooms
1 onion
2 cloves garlic
200 g risotto rice
salt and pepper
500 ml vegetable stock
60 g parmesan
1 glass white wine

The porcini lay dry and wrinkled, each slice twisted by thirst and the colour of parched earth. When the water finally fell, at first only in splashes, they drank what they could, but soon they were all covered with the life-giving liquid. The parched fragments recovered an earlier form, their contortions changed, by the gift of water, into a supine mass, glistening. What had resembled a bowl of tree bark now had the rich colour of cooked meat, the purple brown of wet soil had replaced the dry plaster of Arizona earth. The cook left them like this to soak for 45 minutes.

The first oil, extra virgin, poured into the heavy-bottomed pan, and as the flame licked at the metal, it grew more liquid. The field mushrooms were cool to the touch. Their thin skin

Mushroom Risotto

and soft white bodies yielded to the knife and the slices piled up on the chopping board. The cook wrinkled her nose as she caught the scent of hot oil and lowered the heat before frying the mushrooms. Their pale flesh soaked up the green liquid, and as the heat surged up through the pan, they turned brown and golden, their once perfect matt surface now shining with an oily sheen.

The heat was now everywhere and irresistible. The fire flared up, steady and unbroken; without a flicker the flame worked at the underside of the pan. The cook wiped her brow with her hand as she turned the mushrooms, browning in the pan. Once ready they were put to one side. Fresh oil was added. The porcini were poured into a sieve; their liquid, dark and brackish, she collected to be used later. Nothing was wasted. The drained porcini slid sizzling into the hot oil, which struggled with the water in their flesh. With a cover the cook muffled the voice of the porcini. The steam condensed on the underside of the lid and dripped back into the pan, recreating the cycle of the rains.

Her scarred and calloused hands peeled the onion and garlic before chopping them finely. She knew the porcini would make it if the pan didn't dry out; the moisture would be needed for the work ahead. When ready, the porcini, too, were set aside and the onion and garlic took their place. Their scent rose like a cloud and the cook stood back, her eyes smarting.

The onion grew transparent and soft and gave of its juices. She covered the vegetables with a lid. They murmured and whimpered until they turned to a soft juicy pap. Then the rice rained down onto the onion and garlic, each drop glistening as it was turned in the oil. A drought rain taking moisture where it fell, the rice began to soak up the liquid. As it was added, the porcini stock made a rushing, bubbling sound, like waves breaking at Pebble Beach, and the white grains began to swell, slowly. Soon the liquid was gone. Seasoning was added, and now the vegetable stock was needed, a little at a time, like the movement of the seasons.

The parmesan cheese was hard and dry. The cook grated what little she had. The cheese grated coarsely, like maize from the thresher; the cheese grated finely, like the first powder snow; the cheese grated in shavings, like the wood thrown up from her husband's plane. She divided the parmesan and mixed half into the nearly cooked rice, along with the mushrooms and porcini. The mixture grew thick, and she poured on a shot of white wine before giving a final stir.

She shared the mixture out carefully in the cracked bowls, and sprinkled on the last of the parmesan. It wasn't meat and potatoes, but at least her family would eat tonight.

Boned Stuffed Poussins

à la Marquis de Sade

2 poussins
85 g butter
1 large onion
110 g button mushrooms, sliced
2 tablespoons finely-chopped fresh parsley
55 g fresh white breadcrumbs
grated rind of a quarter of a lemon
30 g prunes, soaked overnight
30 g dried apricots, soaked overnight
salt and freshly ground black pepper
half a beaten egg
170 g mixed chopped onion, turnip, carrot and celery
290 ml chicken stock
1 bay leaf
watercress to garnish

Should not the supreme aim of gastronomy be to untangle the confusion of ideas that confront mankind, and to provide this unfortunate biped with some guidance as to how he should conduct himself and his appetites? Buffeted continually by the studies of scientists, the inventions of dieticians, the fashions of restaurateurs and the disguised marketing campaigns of a thousand trade associations, his own tastes are often his last point of reference. The tyranny

C. 05

Boned Stuffed Poussins

of political correctness, undermining him further, makes of him a man who avoids endangered species, factory farming, deforestation, genetic modification and inhumane slaughter. If he is unfortunate enough also to have a religion, then he will probably live the meanest of lives in the most tightly fitting of gastronomic straitjackets. By walking such a culinary tightrope, he believes that he will reap his rewards in long life, good health, moral superiority and in heaven hereafter. Yet all around him our unfortunate sees good vegetarians pushing up daisies, teetotallers' hearts tightening and sugarphobes queueing in dentists' waiting rooms. Reader, recognise that all your years of abstinence and your naive trust in low-fat yoghurt have not saved you from a pot belly, heavy jowls and an inadequate sex drive. A life of dieting has rendered your face pinched and furrowed from harsh judgement of your fellow diners and your evenings long and lonely.

Not all of our revered chefs eat the food that they recommend so strongly to us and there are many whose appetites are best expressed behind closed doors. It is with these observations in mind that we take up our pen, and in consideration of their wisdom we ask of you, reader, your full attention for this recipe which I recommend to you, told to me by an innocent girl, Justine, who recently had the good fortune to come under my tutelage.

à la Marquis de Sade

Judge Hugon was one of these high priests of abstinence,
and his table was noted for its correctness. Dressed only in
black and white, his visits to the local church struck fear into
the preacher, who felt the eye of the judge upon him as if the
Almighty himself were standing in judgement. The judge
was noted for his rectitude in all matters and his home,
frequented by lawyers and politicians, was a fortress of political
correction. The judge had taken a vow of abstinence from all
unworthy food: endangered cod, non line-caught tuna, prawns
farmed amid the destruction of mangrove swamps and the
meat of all living creatures possessed of a soul. Finally, the
further to set him apart from his fellow men, his wife, once in
possession of three fine children, had invited him to sleep in
the guest room.

One afternoon a knock at the door disturbed the judge
from his correspondence. He found on the doorstep a timid-
looking girl, her delicate countenance a picture of modesty.
Her virginal air and large blue eyes, clear complexion,
bright white teeth and beautiful blonde hair demonstrated
a candour and good faith that were sure to lead her into
trouble. This charming young girl was, in fact, the daughter
of the local butcher and, when her father's deliveryman
had been taken ill at work, in good faith she had offered
her services. Unfamiliar with the poor script of her father's
employee, she had misread an address and now found

Boned Stuffed Poussins

herself, not at number 27 The Avenue, home of a well-known bon viveur, but instead delivering two fine poussins to number 21, residence of a man who had renounced all pleasures involving flesh. This is her tale as she told it to me:

"The house was grand and at the end of a long drive bordered on both sides by a high hedge. The black door looked so grand, in fact, that I was quite in awe and, knowing that I was very late with the deliveries, due to my misfortune in the residents' parking area, I was little prepared for the stern figure who opened the door to me. 'Oh sir, I am sorry to be so late with your poussins. My van was clamped and I have had to finish the last of the deliveries on foot.' I must have looked exhausted from my exertions and my voice seemed to touch a chord in the judge. 'Sweet child, I forgive you,' he said breathlessly. 'Won't you come in and drink something?' Looking left and right, he took the package from me and showed me into a long hall. It was not cold in the house but I noticed that he was trembling as he closed the door. 'I'm sure we can deal with the clamp on your van.' The judge made me answer a number of questions, while he listened with an air of great piety. 1. Was his house definitely the last delivery of the day? 2. Was it true that I was not expected back promptly at my father's shop? 3. Was I sure that once the deliveries were over I was to take the day off? 4. Had I parked the van well away from the house?

"When I had fully satisfied him on these points he seemed to relax. 'There, there, my child, so you won't be missed for a while, and we have plenty of time to deal with these birds, I mean, deal with your stranded vehicle. Let me make a quick telephone call; my office has few benefits, but I am, I hope, not without some power in dealing with your current predicament.'

"He was a very large man, closely shaved with pale skin and piercing grey eyes, and for some reason I was beginning to regret accepting his help. 'I have troubled you enough already, sir; I will walk back to the shop and tell my father.' This seemed to make him angry: 'Are you afraid of a member of Her Majesty's bench? Do you doubt that I would act in any way but that which is most just? How dare you.' With that, he grasped my wrist and shoved me into what appeared to be the pantry. I heard the door being locked from outside and found myself alone in the dark. I banged on the door shouting for help but when there was no response I gave up my cries. As my eyes adjusted to the darkness I could see I was in a small storeroom, lined with shelves on which stood well-ordered packages of wholewheat pasta, boxes of GMO-free oats, packets of rice crackers and jars of sugar-free jam. Noticing the keyhole, I bent down to look through. The sight that met my eyes left me trembling. 'Oh, holy father, am I to be the victim of my good nature and daughterly devotion?'

Boned Stuffed Poussins

"Outside, the judge was slowly peeling away the wrapping to reveal two fleshy white birds, breasts uppermost. I saw his eyes widen and he began talking to the two poussins. 'What have we here? Two naughty little birds.' As he spoke he gave one of them a playful slap. 'We will need to teach you a lesson.' Placing a hand on each bird he gave them a squeeze. 'You have nothing to fear, my little chicks; it is I who am corrupted. Whilst I will break my vow before heaven and must expect the harshest judgement, your innocent souls perch in paradise.'

"He then began to bone the poussins with a kitchen knife. I'm sure my father must have done this on many occasions but I had never watched before. The judge was labouring over the task and sweat dripped from his forehead onto the plump white birds. The job took him some time and he strained and grunted as he worked, using such language that you will forgive me if I refrain from reporting every word of his frightful discourse. Reaching a pause he looked up from his work towards the pantry from which I witnessed his abuses while trembling for my own safety, and he appeared to address the poussins: 'Now, my chicks, you have been well and truly boned. But there is so much more that we can do; how about a little stuffing?' And he took a packet of butter and placed a lump into a pan to melt over a low heat while the villain chopped a large onion. He proceeded to cook the onion gently and then added some sliced button mushrooms. As I watched him, now chopping a bunch of parsley, the odour of the food began to drift in through the keyhole and as, my appetite reminded me that I had not eaten since breakfast, I momentarily forgot my predicament.

"I was soon reminded of my situation when my captor began muttering to himself. Although I could not hear him clearly I caught the words 'fresh, white, succulent fruit,' and nearly fainted with fear when I saw him walking towards my prison door. I covered my eyes and instinctively cowered on the floor. The door opened and I felt his footsteps as he entered the pantry. Then I heard the clink of glass, and the door slammed shut again as he left. Had my sobs roused some mercy in this monster? I looked through the keyhole, expecting to see him doubting his vile course of action, but was instead greeted by the sight of him arranging three jars on the worktop: prunes, dried apricots and breadcrumbs. He added the breadcrumbs and a good handful of the chopped parsley to the onion mixture, before grating some lemon rind on top and stirring in the chopped dried fruits. He added salt and pepper and, finally, the beaten egg.

"All the time the judge's eyes seemed crazed by a deep hunger that had cast aside his judgement leaving only a determination to satisfy his bodily appetites without check or hindrance; I trembled as I witnessed this eruption. The white

Boned Stuffed Poussins

shirt that had seemed so well laundered was now splattered with blood and butter stains. I watched, horrified, as he licked the beaten egg from his fingers and then wiped them down his shirt. If he had answered the door in such a state he could never have taken advantage of my naivety. He now laid the two poussins down in front of him and began to stuff them with the mixture. I had no idea that a small bird could take so much stuffing, but he carried on, using language that my ears could barely suffer, until the poor birds could take no more. Then he took a needle and thread, sewed up their openings and patted the brutalised creatures back into shape. He dropped another knob of butter into a large flameproof dish, and as it foamed with the heat, browned the poussins lightly all over. Meanwhile, the villain had chopped some winter vegetables – onion, turnip, carrot and celery – and these he exchanged in the pan for the now golden poussins, and added a little more butter. I could not see clearly but believe that once the vegetables were lightly browned he placed the poussins back into the pan and added some chicken stock. I was horrified to see him do this using a stock cube; if the old scoundrel had not been in such a hurry he could have made a bouillon using the chicken bones. He added a bay leaf and seasoning and then covered the pan and allowed it to simmer for three quarters of an hour. I must have fainted, for, when I next opened my eyes, the cooked poussins were being placed à la Marquis de Sade

in the oven to keep warm, and Judge Hugon was passing the vegetables through a sieve to extract their juice. He discarded what was left of the crushed vegetables and continued boiling the liquid. I gathered from his study of the spoon that he was waiting for it to take on a honey consistency.

"I feared that once this miserable creature had satisfied the most pressing of his desires it would not be long before this excess of debauchery would overflow and I should become the dish that would feed his baser appetites. I saw that a small ventilation panel high in the pantry might be forced open if I could reach it and disguise the noise of my escape. Climbing up the shelves, I began screaming to be let out and throwing boxes of low sodium salt and soya milk to the ground. As I suspected, my abductor remained engrossed in his stuffed birds and cared not a whit. At the same time I began striking at the ventilation panel using a tin of vegetarian paté. At last the mesh gave way; as the light flooded in I could see below me on the pantry floor a pool of white liquid made up of soya milk and rice drinks running under the door. Wasting no time I squeezed my shoulders through the gap and wriggled my legs through behind me. I found myself in the space between two houses. From fear and relief, I could barely stand; I headed for the neighbour's house, on the door of which a small plaque read 'Sir Michael Mead, MP'; here, surely, was somebody of authority who could help a poor maiden in distress and would see that the judge got his just desserts. I rang the doorbell and fainted."

You may well imagine the politician's distress on finding this poor creature on his doorstep, her clothes stained and her pulse weak. As Justine recovered her senses on his couch, the member of parliament comforted the unfortunate girl as she watered the fine fabric of his soft furnishings with her tears, until they had run their course and she was able to recount the unspeakable happenings of that day. As she spoke, the kindly man took pains to remove all trace of her suffering: the most delicate morsels were served to restore her strength, and while her clothes were taken to be washed, he arranged for the release of her father's delivery vehicle. By the time that Justine left the residence of the honourable member, assured that the accusations against Judge Hugon would be more successfully pursued by a man of influence such as himself, she felt sure in the knowledge that she had found a protector, a man of power with a good heart and respect for those weaker than himself.

No scandal followed, nor was the judge's reputation damaged in any way. Shortly after these events he was appointed Master of the Rolls, and his neighbour, the honourable member, was made a government minister. The two men were both influential at a local level and offered their support to a successful supermarket chain seeking to open a large branch in the elegant neighbourhood. Within a *à la* Marquis de Sade

short time Justine's father's shop had failed, and with it his health. His devoted daughter was obliged to take on evening work in a fried chicken take-away establishment. And so it was that I had the good fortune to discover her there, late one night.

You, who have shed a tear for the misfortune of one so virtuous, you, who pity the unfortunate Justine, take comfort. If, through forces that it is not given us to understand, God allows her to be persecuted on earth, it is in order to compensate her all the more in heaven hereafter.

Clafoutis Grandmère

à la Virginia Woolf

500 g cherries
100 g butter
150 g sugar
3 eggs
150 g flour
10 g yeast, prepared in warm water if necessary
1 cup of milk

She placed the cherries in a buttered dish and looked out
of the window. The children were racing across the lawn,
Nicholas already between the clumps of red-hot pokers,
turning to wait for the others. Looking back at the cherries,
that would not be pitted, red polka dots on white, so bright
and jolly, their little core of hardness invisible, in pity she
thought of Mrs Sorley, that poor woman with no husband and
so many mouths to feed, Mrs Sorley who knew the hard core
but not the softness; and she placed the dish of cherries to
one side.

Gently she melted the butter, transparent and smooth,
oleaginous and clear, clarified and golden, and mixed it with
the sugar in a large bowl. Should she have made something
traditionally English? (Involuntarily, piles of cake rose before
her eyes.) Of course the recipe was French, from her
grandmother. English cooking was an abomination: it was

Clafoutis Grandmère

boiling cabbages in water until they were liquid; it was roasting meat until it was shrivelled; it was cutting out the flavours with a blunt knife.

She added an egg, pausing to look up at the jacmanna, its colour so vivid against the whitewashed wall. Would it not be wonderful if Nicholas became a great artist, all life stretching before him, a blank canvas, bright coloured shapes gradually becoming clearer? There would be lovers, triumphs, the colours darkening, work, loneliness, struggle. She wished he could stay as he was now, they were so happy; the sky was so clear, they would never be as happy again. With great serenity she added an egg, for was she not descended from that very noble, French house whose female progeny brought their arts and energy, their sense of colour and shape, wit and poise to the sluggish English? She added an egg, whose yellow sphere, falling into the domed bowl, broke and poured, like Vesuvius erupting into the mixture, like the sun setting into a butter sea. Its broken shell left two uneven domes on the counter, and all the poverty and all the suffering of Mrs Sorley had turned to that, she thought.

When the flour came it was a delight, a touch left on her cheek as she brushed aside a wisp of hair, as if her beauty bored her and she wanted to be like other people, insignificant, sitting in a widow's house with her pen and paper, writing notes, understanding the poverty, revealing the social problem (she folded the flour into the mixture). She was so commanding (not tyrannical, not domineering; she should not have minded what people said), she was like an arrow set on a target. She would have liked to build a hospital, but how? For now, this clafoutis for Mrs Sorley and her children (she added the yeast, prepared in warm water). The yeast would cause the mixture to rise up into the air like a column of energy, nurtured by the heat of the oven, until the arid kitchen knife of the male, cutting mercilessly, plunged itself into the dome, leaving it flat and exhausted.

Little by little she added the milk, stopping only when the mixture was fluid and even, smooth and homogenous, lumpless and liquid, pausing to recall her notes on the iniquity of the English dairy system. She looked up: what demon possessed him, her youngest, playing on the lawn, demons and angels? Why should it change, why could they not stay as they were, never ageing? (She poured the mixture over the cherries in the dish.) The dome was now become a circle, the cherries surrounded by the yeasty mixture that would cradle and cushion them, the yeasty mixture that surrounded them all, the house, the lawn, the asphodels, that devil Nicholas running past the window, and she put it in a hot oven. In thirty minutes it would be ready.

Fenkata

à la Homer

1 rabbit
extra virgin olive oil
rabbit herbs (2 sprigs each of thyme and rosemary, and
*   a handful of flat-leaf parsley, all roughly chopped)*
75 ml red wine
2 onions
3 cloves of garlic
10 fresh plum tomatoes, peeled
1 tablespoon tomato puree
2 medium potatoes, peeled and chopped into small pieces
2 carrots, peeled and chopped
a handful of peas, preferably petit pois
2 bay leaves
seasoning

Sing now, goddess, of the hunger of Peleus' son, Achilles.
Tell me now, you Muses of Olympia, daughters of Zeus, of the
empty-bellied Achaians, whose supplies were grown old and
stagnant while they stormed the great walls of Ilion for ten
long years. You who know all things, while we have heard
only the rumour of it and know nothing, tell me now of the
cunning of resourceful Odysseus who, when he saw the
hunger that spread through the strong-greaved Achaians,
as obliterating fire lights up a vast forest along the crest of a

mountain, was not dismayed, but stood forward to take up his bow and his cauldron of bronze.

Now, when rosy-fingered dawn showed, Odysseus stirred from where he was sleeping and slung his bow over his shoulder. He bound the fair sandals beneath his shining feet and went on his way into the sand dunes. Soon he came upon a swift-footed coney grazing in the dunes, and now Odysseus the godlike, holding his bow and his quiver full of arrows, bent the bow before him and let the arrow fly. Nor was his aim untrue, but Apollo, who strikes from afar, was still angry with the strong-greaved Achaians and sent the arrow astray so that it fell harmlessly in the sand. Now the startled rabbit began to run to take cover, swiftly as a mountain stream, which gains speed before disappearing beneath the glistening rock, only to appear later in some unexpected place. But Athene appeared to Odysseus and told him to shoot a second arrow, though it seemed hopeless; and this time he did not waste his strength; the bronze-weighted arrow found its mark and passed through the liver and came out the other side and undid the strength of the rabbit's legs, and its black blood drenched the sand and its eyes were shrouded in darkness.

Odysseus bound the mighty creature's feet and slung him over his shoulder to carry back to the Achaians' camp on the beach of the grey sea, beneath the bows of the wooden ships.

à la Homer

Then swift-footed brilliant Achilles gave up his weeping and came out from his tent. He girt about his chest and loins a leather apron and skinned the rabbit and cut it expertly into equal parts. Then he took the pieces and fried them in olive oil until they were brown and the smoke rose up to high Olympus, where sit the gods who rule over men. Seeing Achilles the godlike no longer brooding in his tent, Menelaos took courage and came with herbs and seasoning, which he added to the cauldron. Then resourceful Odysseus mixed the sweet wine in the bowl and poured it over the meat and removed the cauldron from the fire, to allow it to marinate for thirty minutes.

Atreus' son, wide-ruling Agamemnon the powerful, chopped the onions and shed tears, as a stream dark, running down the face of a cliff impassable, sheds its dim water; but raging that it was not king-like, he would chop no more. Now Achilles chopped the garlic and, in a separate cauldron given by Agamemnon, fried the onions and garlic, nor did he stop frying until the onions began to brown. Then he added the tomatoes, the puree, the vegetables and the bay leaves to heat and simmer for fifteen minutes. Now Nestor the wise, with the guidance of Athene, persuaded them to combine the contents of the two cauldrons into one. This they left to simmer over a cool part of the fire for one hour, so that the rabbit was soft and tender. Then Achilles offered up a prayer to mighty Zeus of the wide brows, and he poured the wine into the mixing bowl and looked up into the sky. "High Zeus in far Olympus, hear me as you have heard me before and did me honour and brought to pass the wish that I prayed for. For see how I myself have worked hard with my hands and cooked the rabbit and made offerings of the vitals. Grant that the food is good and that my work is appreciated by the Achaians, and not only when my hands rage invincible against the Trojans, and that the meal will be eaten in good spirit without dispute among the lords of the glancing-eyed Achaians." So he spoke in prayer, and Zeus of the wise counsel heard the son of Peleus and granted him one prayer but not the other. That the food should be good he allowed, but refused to let the meal pass in harmony.

But resourceful Odysseus was mindful of the appetites of the Achaians, and when the dish was ready he took the sauce to serve on platters over linguini as a starter. Now Agamemnon stood forward and claimed the biggest portion, "Since I am king and greater than all here so that no man may contend with me." He spoke thus and then sat down, and the anger came on war-like Achilles, so that his heart was divided two ways, whether to take up his sword and kill Agamemnon or whether to put aside his anger and serve him the worst portion. Then in answer spoke Achilles unto Agamemnon, lord of men. "You wine sack with a dog's appetite, my portion you threaten to reduce for which I laboured much. When the

Achaians cook, do I have a share that is equal to yours?
Though always the greater part of the cooking is the work of
my hands, when the time comes to dispense the rations, yours
is the far greater reward."

　　Now Nestor the horseman stood forth among them and
spoke to them saying, "Proud Achilles, beyond others you are
strong in battle, not one of all the Achaians will belittle your
words nor speak against them, yet you have not completed
your arguments. But let me speak, since I am older, and go
through the whole matter, since there is none who can
dishonour the thing I say. I will speak in the way it seems best
to my mind, and no one shall have in his mind any thought
that is better than this one that I have in my mind, either now
or long before now. Let lots be shaken for all of you to see who
wins which portion." So he spoke and each of them marked
one lot as his own. They threw them in the helmet of Atreus'
son Agamemnon. And Achilles set before each of them a
portion, according to their lot. Nor was any man's hunger
denied, and they put their hands forward to the good things
that lay before them and ate until they had put away the desire
for eating and drinking.

Vietnamese Chicken

à la Graham Greene

3 cloves garlic
1/2 teaspoon grated lemon zest
2 tablespoons fish sauce
1 tablespoon soy sauce
1 teaspoon finely ground black pepper
1/8 teaspoon cayenne
2 boneless chicken breasts
2 tablespoons dry sherry
1 teaspoon molasses
2 tablespoons lemon juice
2 tablespoons peanut oil

A recipe has no beginning or end: arbitrarily one chooses
at what point the cooking instructions become necessary, after
the butcher has done his work and before care of the dish
passes to the seasoning whims of the guests. I choose
the moment when, looking into the refrigerator, I noticed
the naked white flesh of the chicken. As I stared at the breasts
I felt a pain across my head. The sound of church bells
announced evensong from across the darkening Common,
and I sipped at a gin and tonic. The tonic was old and had lost
its sparkle, leaving a bitter taste, but it was now too late to get
anything fresher. The rain drove against the window, and water
was collecting on the sill where it refused to close.

... I acknowledge my transgressions: and my sins es
ever before me.

Vietnamese Chicken

The smell of chopped garlic clung to my hands as I mixed it together with the lemon zest, fish and soy sauces, and the peppers, black and cayenne. The chicken breasts rested on the counter and my hand moved towards them as though guided by an unseen force. It was too late to go back; she would be here soon.

Ritually I sliced the breasts into thin strips. The white flesh lay on the plate like a shredded contract and I hurriedly threw it into the marinade. The soy and fish sauce splashed across the meat, like ink smudged in the wet. I covered the mixture and returned it to the refrigerator. Two more hours would be ideal, but if the chicken soaked for half an hour it would be all right. I thought that in future I must do better.

While the flesh marinated in the cold darkness I mixed together the sherry, molasses and lemon juice. I poured another gin, without tonic this time, and turned on the wireless. The choral music was interrupted by a reading, Psalm 51. I turned off the set, but I knew the reading and it continued silently in my head as I heated the oil in the wok until it was smoking.

I took the marinated breasts from the refrigerator and tipped them into the burning oil, turning them with a fork. When the chicken was almost ready I added the sherry sauce; the rich liquid thickening made a sharp contrast to the whiteness of the steamed rice I would serve with it. I had failed

à la Graham Greene

to wear an apron, and as I stirred more rapidly, the rich concoction splashed onto my white shirt. I wiped at it with a cloth but the stain grew worse. In my frustration I called out "Damned . . .", but before I could finish I was interrupted by a knock at the door.

Sole à la Dieppoise

à la Jorge Luis Borges

¹/₂ litre mussels
2 fillets of sole
100 g button mushrooms
50 g butter
half a lemon
125 ml white wine
1 tablespoon plain flour

The story that I shall tell concerns an incident that took place in London early in 1945. Its protagonist was proclaimed a hero by both sides of the conflict, yet its consequences favoured only one, and led to the downfall of a seemingly invincible tyrant with an insatiable appetite.

Early in the Second World War, fearing invasion, the British removed all signposts from their highways. The intention was that spies and invaders would find themselves lost in the endless labyrinth of Celtic curves that make up much of the British road network. The task of overseeing the project fell to Sir Henry Smith. Inspired by the British initiative, a Parisian restaurateur, Amadée Antonin, removed the place names from all dishes on the menu of his small hostelry. For a short while, German officers dining in Antonin's restaurant found themselves lost in a recondite menu without signposts. The entries for such dishes as Crayfish à la Bordelaise and Lobster

Sole à la Dieppoise

à la Parisienne offered the diner no guidance as to the possible fates of the unfortunate decapods, and Paris Brest could only be ordered by those who had known the menu since childhood.

It was in the old Confiteria Aguila that I first came across Sir Henry Smith's story. A small item in the Buenos Aires journal Carne y Produccion noted the anniversary of his death and gave brief details of his career. Later, during a lecture tour of Germany, I stumbled upon another report of Sir Henry Smith or of a second Sir Henry Smith. Here the story grew deeper and more complicated. The article concerned papers from the wartime government, only recently released, in which reference was made to Sir Henry as 'The Spying Knight of the Reich', German intelligence's highest-placed agent during the Second World War.

My lecture tour moved on to England and there I spent much of my free time researching the strange history of Sir Henry. From privileged access to the journal of his last days, written in the cuneiform he had learnt as Woolley's amanuensis at Sumerian Ur, I have tried to create a full picture of his final hours, faithful to the facts where they were available. As may be expected I will alter one or two details. Here is his story.

It was on March 2nd 1944, at 1 pm precisely, that Sir Henry Smith turned into Great College Street and, before the chime *à la* Jorge Luis Borges

of Big Ben had faded on the air, remembered the note that he had been handed as he left the House of Commons. Sir Henry read the single line that occupied the page. Fearing that he might faint, he steadied himself against a wall and refused an offer of help from a passer-by. The note was from his contact, Agent 42, who had recently been directing Sir Henry to pay particular attention to information that might indicate the location of a probable Allied invasion of France.

The imminent capture of Agent 42 inferred Sir Henry's own arrest and execution. In the few minutes required to walk home, and from the infinite choices that lay before him, Sir Henry decided upon his plan of action. From the small bookshelf in the kitchen he took down a little-thumbed volume and his glacial eyes began to scan the index: Cod à l'Anglaise, Cod Provençal, Crayfish à la Bordelaise, Fish Soup à la Nimoise, Sole à la Dieppoise. Satisfied, Sir Henry scribbled a note that he passed to the concierge with a large tip and instructions that the fish was not to be filleted.

Sir Henry, feeling the relief of a murderer who finds himself under arrest, sat on the sofa by the bookcase. He opened a volume at random and began to read. The pages told the story of Astyages, whose merciless numina had brought to him the rule of Persia, and who defined his invincible purpose through the dream interpretations of the Magi. On their advice Astyages ordered the death of his own grandchild. When his

Sole à la Dieppoise

orders were frustrated by the disobedience of his general, Harpagus, Astyages butchered the latter's son and served him cooked to the nescient father. At the end of the meal the boy's head and hands were brought to the table. Harpagus made no show of revolt, but in secret sent a message, hidden in the stomach of a cooked hare, to Astyages' (now fully-grown) grandson, Cyrus, promising the general's collusion in any attempt to overthrow the tyrant. Fearing discovery, Harpagus sent a second message, concealed in the boiled carcass of a turtle, urging all speed, which arrived before the first and gave rise to the apocryphal tale of the Greek fabulist.

The book grew heavy and Sir Henry fell into a sleep. He was visited by the same dream that had recurred at intervals over the preceding months. He found himself in a vast maze, whose creator was observing from a tower as the dreamer ran through the green corridors of the rain-drenched labyrinth, trying, unsuccessfully, to take an unseen direction or to make an unpredicted move. Sir Henry was awoken by the return of the concierge, whose trip had been a success. He left the minister with a pint of mussels and a single sole, with the spine still attached.

Sir Henry was neither an accomplished cook nor an habitual piscivore, but he prided himself that, as a loyal servant, he knew how to follow instructions. Opening the recipe book, he cleaned the mussels and left them to stand in a à la Jorge Luis Borges

bowl of fresh water while he made a telephone call to a journalist on *The Times*. Reports tell us that the journalist agreed to come to Sir Henry's apartment at 8 o'clock that evening, on the understanding that the minister had a story for him. Sir Henry then seasoned the sole with salt and pepper and placed the pieces in a flameproof pan. The sun had by now descended below the rooftops and through the window he perceived the tower of Westminster Abbey. The light of the gas flame took over from the extravagant sunset and illuminated Sir Henry's irremeable countenance. He drained the mussels and recovered them with the fresh water so alien to their nature, discarding as irretrievable any that did not close when tapped. He fried the mushrooms in a little butter and squeezed some lemon juice over them, covering the pan to preserve the juices. Meanwhile, he redrained the shellfish and placed the covered pan over a gentle heat, shaking it gently until all the bivalves were open, again removing any that did not conform with the majority. Sir Henry drained the liquid into a bowl and removed the mussels from their shells. The mushrooms were now ready and he poured the liquid from their pan over the sole, then added a glass of white wine and the juice from the mussels, so that there was just enough liquid to cover the fish.

Among the unread books in Sir Henry's library sat Augustine of Trieste's treatise on asceticism. Confronted with a meal of fish, Augustine postulates the argument against

Sole à la Dieppoise

carnivorism. Once eaten, the fish would transubstantiate into the flesh of the anathematised eater, and, for Augustine, to whom this fish was Sir Henry's own ancestor, its consumption was no less than cannibalism. He brought the liquid to simmering point and poached the sole with measured chronometry. On the stroke of the eighth minute Sir Henry lifted the sole from the liquid and placed it onto a warmed serving dish. He surrounded the fish with the mussels and fried mushrooms and kept it warm while he reduced the poaching liquid by allowing it to boil for three minutes and 30 seconds. Meanwhile, Sir Henry facilitated the collaboration of the remaining butter and flour, which he interpolated gradually into the liquid, stirring continually until the sauce thickened. He thought of the infinite possibilities of these few ingredients and of the practicability of cookery being classified as a branch of mathematics, rejecting this hypothesis in favour of gastronomy as language. He poured the sauce over the fish and placed the dish under a hot grill for a few moments to brown, before serving it with mashed potato.

Debate concerning the actual ingredients employed is of a dialectical nature. The recipe book used by Sir Henry disappeared following the inquest but is likely to have been the spuriously modernised 1921 edition of *Baron Brisse's 366 Menus*. From the depositions of the concierge and of the journalist, I can hope to have reconstructed the recipe with a fair degree of accuracy.

Sir Henry poured a glass of white wine to accompany his meal, took the front door off the latch and sat down at the table. As the firmament grew dark and the Abbey disintegrated into the gloom, he conjectured that he would not have the honour of facing the opprobrium of his countrymen. The chimes of Big Ben could be heard as the clock struck the hour, and recalling other ancient evenings, Sir Henry offered up a short prayer before beginning his lustral supper.

He was found later that evening by the visiting journalist, his lean, athletic figure sprawled across the carpet, arms outstretched. On the table were the remains of a meal half-eaten and an open recipe book. The following day the late edition of *The Times* ran the headline MINISTER FOUND DEAD. Along with the title of the dish that he had been eating, the journalist had interpolated the detail that Sir Henry's throat had been lacerated by fish bones as he choked to death. Five days later a German infantry regiment was moved from the Normandy coast to a defensive position in the environs of Dieppe, and the first glowing obituaries had already appeared in honour of Sir Henry Smith.

Cheese on Toast
à la Harold Pinter

1 loaf of ciabatta
1 aubergine
extra virgin olive oil
pesto
200 g mozzarella
2 teaspoons fresh oregano, chopped

ACT I

A kitchen, cluttered. A fluorescent tube is flickering, trying to light. Beneath a window is a sink, piled with dirty dishes. The bin is overflowing with rubbish; nearby, empty bottles are standing. There is a small kitchen table; newspapers and unopened letters obscure the surface. At the table are two chairs. There is the sound of a key in a door, muffled voices. The door bangs shut; instantly HURLEY, a young man dressed in a leather jacket, and CLACK, an older man, tramp-like in appearance, enter stage left.

HURLEY. Come in, make yourself at home.
  (CLACK *enters and looks around*)
  Bloody light. I've been meaning to get a new tube.
  (HURLEY *reaches up and taps the light with his finger until it stops flickering.*) I'll make you something to eat.
CLACK. I haven't eaten all day. I can't remember the last time I

had a proper meal. I mean a proper sit-down meal, something hot.

HURLEY. (*Looking in the fridge*) Do you want to use the phone? Call your daughter?

CLACK. What, at this time? I'll call her tomorrow. She won't want to come up here tonight, she starts early in the morning.

HURLEY. I can't offer you much. I haven't done a proper shop for ages. How about cheese on toast?

CLACK. What sort of cheese?

HURLEY. Mozzarella.

CLACK. Mozza what?

HURLEY. Mozzarella. It's Italian.

CLACK. Not for me. I'll have a slice of toast though.

Pause

HURLEY. I must wash this grill sometime.

(*He is holding a grill pan covered with dried cooked cheese. He cuts a ciabatta in half, lengthways. Similarly, he finely slices an aubergine and puts the pieces into a frying pan where some oil is heating.*)

CLACK. Not a bad little place you got here. All yours is it?

Pause

This must be worth a few bob. How long you been here?

HURLEY. I don't know . . . about three years.

CLACK. Made a few bob on it, have you?

(HURLEY *puts the ciabatta under the grill to warm*)

That's a big slice of toast.

HURLEY. It's ciabatta.

CLACK. Cia what?

HURLEY. Ciabatta. It's Italian bread.

CLACK. You Italian are you?

HURLEY. Everybody eats it these days: ciabatta, focaccia, schiacciata, panini.

CLACK. Can't you just put me a couple of slices in the toaster?

HURLEY. Toaster's broken.

Pause

I'd like to have a little Italian eatery one day. Nothing fancy, mind. Simple snacks: panini on ciabatta, focaccia, bruschetta; pasta lunches, spaghetti, penne, rigatoni; the basic sauces, pesto, Bolognese, arrabiata. Classic mains: carpaccio of tuna drizzled with truffle oil, pan-fried fillet of beef on a bed of wilted spinach in its own jus. You want a cup of tea with it?

CLACK. Now you're talking. A nice cup of tea.

HURLEY. You ever been to Italy? I knew a bloke there once, bit like you. That was years ago. He's probably dead by now.

(*He removes the aubergine from the pan, the flesh has soaked up the oil and is a golden colour with dark stripes left by the ridges of the frying pan. The ciabatta has now warmed and he spreads a thin layer of pesto onto the cut side*). Where's your daughter live then?

CLACK. My what?

HURLEY. Your daughter. The one who was meant to pick you up at the station.

CLACK. Oh her.

Pause

She lives in Catford.

HURLEY. Catford? I used to go to the dogs there. I remember one night I was doing well, nearly all winners I'd picked, till I put the lot on the last race. I did a forecast, two and four. I don't know why, I nearly always did two and four about. But that night I didn't. Only came in four and two. I lost the lot. You a gambler?

CLACK. What, and throw my money away like that? Not me.

(*Pause as he looks down at his lap*)

You haven't got a safety pin have you?

(HURLEY *lays the slices of aubergine on top of the ciabatta and pesto and begins to slice the mozzarella.*)

HURLEY. You can give her a call in the morning. I'll make you a bed up.

CLACK. She works in the morning. I told you.

HURLEY. You like olive oil?

(*He lays the mozzarella over the aubergine, drizzles olive oil on top, and finally adds a sprinkle of chopped oregano, before placing the ciabatta under a hot grill.*)

CLACK. I don't want none of that foreign muck.

HURLEY. Olive oil? It's good for you.

CLACK. It's for cleaning your ears out, ain't it?

HURLEY. (*Drops a tea bag into the overflowing bin*) Here you are, a cup of tea for you.

CLACK. (*Gives a sigh of contentment*) You can't beat a nice cup of tea.

(*He sips at the tea and pulls a face*)

You got any sugar?

HURLEY. Over there, on the table. I don't use it much.
(*The sugar has hardened. CLACK chips at it with a teaspoon until he has sweetened his tea enough. He checks it occasionally throughout the process. The sound of sizzling comes from the grill. HURLEY waits until the mozzarella has turned brown and golden in places.*)

HURLEY. Here you are. It's ready.

(HURLEY *cuts the two lengths of ciabatta into pieces.*)

You'll try some, won't you?

CLACK. Not for me. That's no good to a man like me.

(HURLEY *puts the plate of ciabatta onto the table.*)

Don't look bad though, I'll give that to you. It's . . .

Pause

Well presented. That's what it is, well presented.

Cheese on Toast

HURLEY. I would have done a salad garnish, or a few fresh
     basil leaves if I'd had them.
CLACK. Don't look bad at all.
     Pause
     I'll just have a taste.
     (*He takes a piece and bites into it. The mozzarella sticks to his
     beard in long threads. His face brightens in surprise.*)
CLACK. That ain't bad, that ain't. I reckon you might make
     a go of that caff yet.
He reaches for a second piece. HURLEY is already eating.
The two men sit in silence, occasionally sipping at their tea.
The fluorescent tube begins to flicker again, but this time
HURLEY ignores it. Lights slowly fade.

Curtain

Onion Tart

à la Geoffrey Chaucer

225 g plain shortcrust pastry
1 tablespoon chopped fresh thyme
25 g butter
2 tablespoons olive oil
8 onions, finely sliced
2 teaspoons caster sugar
salt and black pepper
$1/4$ teaspoon each of grated nutmeg and ground ginger
425 ml double cream
large pinch of saffron strands
2 eggs, plus 2 egg yolks

Then spake oure Host.
"Now have we heard from every which one
Of our fellowship with receipts to tell, but one.
Maister Graham, as knoweth many a man,
Loves best tales of cuckoldry as he kan.
And thou, wyfe of Bloomesbury, long of face,
Right boldly hast thou taken thy place.
God knowes well thy stream of consciousnesse,
For your clafoutis may God you blesse.
And thou, clerke of Prague, put away thy bookes,
Tis no time for Ovid, our tales are for cookes.
Culinary are our metamorphoses,
From ingredients chaos, creators we.

Onion Tart

And when such tellers as these turn their voices cleere,
To Ars Culinaria, as they have here,
Nourished are our Christian men's soules,
But no less our bellies, our board and bowls.
And thou, sire at excise, who hath herkened these tales,
All the while taking note and drinking ale,
Telle us some merry dish, by your fay,
For 'tis high time thou entreth in the play."
"Gladly", quod he,
"Certe I can roaste and seethe and broille and frye,
But, as it thinketh me, nought can best a pie.
Therefore I will go tell, as well as ever I kan,
A receipt that will nourishe us, every man.
Now herkneth what I saye.

Here beginneth the Man at Excise's receipt:
On a floured board roll pastry that it be thinne,
Caste thereto with thyme and line a deep tinne.
Trimme the edges neat with a cooke's knyfe,
Then bake it blinde at gasse mark fyve.
Melt the butter and oyle in an heavie panne,
Covered wiv a lidde, as knoweth every man.
Then adde onyons in slices fine ywrought,
And caste thereto sugar and salte.
Cover the panne and turn the heat down low,

Onion Tart

Stirre every while, else the onyons stick to.
Remove the lidde and seethe for ten minutes mo,
That the sauce reducteth and darke growe.
Strewe thereto nutmeg grated, tho keep some by,
And grounde gyngere, and return to the fyre.
Lightly beat the eggs and zolkes together,
And season wiv both salt and black pepper.
Heat the crème till just warme with saffron rich,
Then adde the beaten eggs for to mix.
Spoon the onyon sauce into the pastry case,
Then pour egg and crème custard into the base.
Bake in the oven for minutes xxv,
Til golden brown our tarte be."
Here endeth the receipt of the Exciseman of London.

"Now", quod our Host, "so God you blesse,
Ye have set an ensample for the rest,
Since ye so much knowen of that art,
And right well have you told us part.
Though in kitchen's cunning there's nought, dear brother,
That in olde tyme was not said by another,
In the way of telling your creation's made,
For none shall remember you by your trade.
Thy customhouse stores much of strange beauty,
And in future with tales will pilgrims pay duty."

THE END